Where Did Everything Come From?

Starring Billy and Bee, Who Are Blue and Green

By
David Misialowski
John MacDonald
Scott Thorson

ISBN
978-1-944854-16-4

Art by
David Misialowski
Scott Thorson

www.poodpawprints.com
facebook.com/poodpawprints
youtube.com/@poodpawprints
instagram.com/poodpawprints

Where did Everything Come From?, Published by Pood Paw Prints, 18819 71st Ave NE, Kenmore WA 98028, United States. This book copyright 2024 By Pood Paw Prints. All rights reserved. No portion of this product may be reproduced or transmitted, by any form or by any means, without the express written permission of Pood Paw Prints.

Chapter One

His name was Billy Brown. But people called him Billy Brain because he was really smart.

It wasn't always meant as a compliment.

"Brain! Brain! Brain!" some of the kids at school teased him. Billy Brain couldn't feel insulted, though. What was wrong with being smart?

Also, even though his last name was Brown, Billy was blue. Not blue as in sad — blue as in skin color. His blue color and his big brain made him stand out, and not in a good way. How many kids do you know who have blue skin? Or big brains? How many have both?

So Billy didn't have many friends. Maybe, because of that, he was a little sad, after all. Maybe his skin was blue because he *was* blue.

Blue or not, he was smart. But did you know that many smart people are sad? That many brains are blue? That many smiles are silent frowns?

He wasn't just smart. He had a great imagination. He found the neighborhood he lived in boring. So he invented a new one. He put in it cranks, wizards, witches, warlocks, monsters, mad scientists and crackpot inventors. He felt less alone that way.

He also invented different time periods for each house. People not only lived in different places, but in different times. Even different centuries.

For example: cranky old Mr. Sour Hour lived in the 19th century. He lived in a haunted house with black bats and black cats. The cats ate the bats, and the bats ate the cats. But both were black, so you couldn't tell who was eating whom.

Mr. Eins Stein lived in the 20th century, in a flying saucer. It orbited the earth. Folks said Mr. Stein was weird because he didn't wear socks. That was because he was an absent-minded professor. He was also German. His name meant "one stein," or "glass" of root beer. You didn't need a rocket to get to Mr. Eins Stein's house. You could get to it by thinking real hard. Billy Brain was good at thinking.

There were others, too. Mr. Darwinkle also lived in the 19th century, on an island. It was populated by the Doppelgängers. They were all exactly alike, except they weren't. He was a moose. A bearded moose.

Mr. Knee Cheese, another 1800s guy, kept a pet walrus above his upper lip. He also owned a horse. Folks said his knees were made of cheese. Folks also said he was crazy.

Mr. Whom lived in the 1700s in a castle. Even though he was in Scotland he was right next door. He was a pronoun. Some people called him Mr. Who, with whom (not who!) he was often confused. Mr. Who was the Who who (whom? English can be weird) Horton heard.

Then there was Mr. Kalamazoo. He was not really a person, but a way of thinking. He was also a city in Michigan. He was a teacher in the Middle Ages, a long time ago. He kept an invisible pink unicorn as a pet.

Oh, there were so many of them! He decided to visit them.

But first, he had to eat his peas.

He had to eat them before Mom and Dad would give him his birthday cake. It had ten candles on it because Billy had just turned ten.

"Eat your peas," Mom said. His little sister, Beatrice, stuck out her tongue at him. A partly eaten pea rolled off the tip of it. It landed on the tablecloth. Seeing that made Billy Brain feel kind of sick.

"Why?" Billy said.

"Because, Billy, your mother said so," said Dad, frowning. Dad frowned A LOT. He was an accountant. Billy thought he was kind of a bore.

Billy made a face. "I don't like peas," he said.

"They're good for you," Mom said.

"Why?"

"Because your mother said so!" Dad said.

"Why is everything I like to eat bad for me? And everything I don't like good for me?"

"Why! Why! Why! All you ever do is ask 'why'!"

"Why not?"

"Why not what?"

"Why not ask 'why?'"

"Oh, Billy, honestly!"

"That's why the other kids call him Billy Brain," said Beatrice. She was being snarky. She didn't think 'Brain' was a compliment, either. She thought it meant you were a nerd.

Which was weird, because Beatrice was also really smart. She was a straight-A pupil in first grade. Sometimes folks called her Brain, too. Beatrice Brain. Although she liked to tease her brother, he was secretly her hero. Her skin wasn't blue, though.

It was green.

Why did she tease her brother? Maybe she was also a little jealous of him. Or maybe not. But, you know, envy makes your skin green. At least, that's what some folks say.

"Billy, eat your peas."

"Where do peas come from?" Billy asked.

"From the ground," his father said.

"Oh," Billy said. "I thought you were going to tell me the stork brought peas."

"No, the stork brought *you*, Billy," Mom said.

"Bullpucky," Billy pouted.

"Billy!"

"Where did everything come from?" Billy suddenly asked.

"Everything?"

"Yes, everything," Billy demanded. "The sun, the moon, the stars, our house, you, me, everything. Where did everything come from?"

"Everything is a gift from God," Mom said.

"Not a stork?"

"No," Dad said, sounding irritated. "God is not a stork. God is God."

"Where did God come from?"

"God didn't come from anywhere," his father said. "God has always been around. Now eat your peas!"

Beatrice stuck out her tongue again at Billy and mimicked her father: "Eat your peas, Billy!"

Billy said, "Maybe you eat too many peas. Maybe that's why you're green. Ever think of that, Bee?" Billy called his sister Bee because it was easier to say than 'Beatrice.' It was also because she buzzed like a bee. She was annoying in that way. Plus, "Bee" rhymes with "pea."

"Maybe," Billy added, "we should call you 'Peatrice.'"

"Ma-a-ham!" Beatrice yelled. "Make Billy stop!"

"Buzz! Buzz! Buzz!" Billy said.

"Billy, stop teasing Beatrice, and eat your peas."

Billy Brain rolled his eyes, but ate his peas. His mother made a video on her phone of Billy eating his peas. "Look, Roy," she told her husband, "Billy is eating his peas."

"Big whoop," Billy mumbled. "Next you'll expect me to eat my carrots, too. Then I might turn orange."

"This is going on Facebook," Mom said. She liked the world to know about her children's wins, like when Billy ate his peas. Billy rolled his eyes again.

Then he got to blow out the ten candles on his birthday cake. After that, he gobbed it all down. It was chocolate. It sure tasted better than the peas.

The next day was Saturday, and Billy didn't have to go to school.

He was happy about that. School bored him.

He decided to get up bright and early and visit his neighbors. Maybe, he thought, they could tell him why he had a big brain. Maybe they could tell him why his sister was a pest. Maybe they could tell him why he was blue, and his sister green.

Maybe they could even tell him where everything came from. And why anything existed at all.

Billy's room

Mr. Whom the balloon

Chapter Two

We said Billy Brain invented a new neighborhood. That means he built it out of scraps.

Billy Brain's neighborhood was scattered about his room. Pieces hung on the walls. They hid behind dropped books. They poked out from under his bed. Colorful scraps of cardboard were held together with string, paperclips, and glue. The cardboard was covered with characters from cereal boxes, toys, and things from the recycling bin. Each told a story that brimmed from Billy's brain.

Mom and Dad thought this was kinda weird, and worried about Billy's behavior. But Dad — being an accountant — was also practical. That means he thought about real-world stuff.

He thought Billy's odd hobby meant that he would become an architect some day. He called it "a practical profession." He and Mom even bought Billy Legos. They thought he could make better little houses and buildings with them.

So Billy's bedroom was filled with cardboard and later Legos. Pretty soon Mom was taking videos of the room with her phone. She put them on Facebook. When she did this, Billy rolled his eyes. He was a real eye-roller.

On Saturday morning, Billy Brain was getting ready to visit his neighbors. Then Beatrice burst into his bedroom.

"Bee!" Billy cried. "Knock first!"

"Not Bee! Beatrice!" In frustration, she flapped her hands at him. It made her look like — well, like a bee. A bee flapping its wings.

"Buzz off, Bee."

"You're planning to visit the neighbors, aren't you?"

"How did you know?"

"I'm you're sister, silly. I know you like a book."

"What if I am?" Billy frowned, folded his arms, and turned his back on her.

"I want to go with you." She clenched her hands in excitement, and bounded up and down on her toes. Billy looked at her again. Her eyes pleaded with him.

"Well, you're not! I don't want my silly little sis tagging along with me. You'll embarrass me!"

"If you don't take me with you, Billy, I'll, I'll … um .. I know! I'll hold my breath until I turn blue."

"You can't turn blue. You're green. I'm blue!"

"Oh," Beatrice said. "Right."

"You can't come."

Beatrice burst into tears. Billy rolled his eyes.

"Okay," he said, shoulders slumping. "You can come. Just don't ask stupid questions, and don't do anything to embarrass me."

"Yay!" His sister cried. They were now sitting together on Billy's bed, and she grabbed his hands in excitement. But then Bee looked around, and frowned.

"Your whole neighborhood is just cardboard and Legos!" she said. "How can we visit anybody inside these toys? Plus, they're too small to enter."

"See how silly you are?" Billy told her. He pointed at a big mirror on the wall. You could see all of Billy's creations reflected in it.

"It's a mirror," Beatrice said. "What about it?"

"It's more than a mirror," Billy said.

"What do you mean?"

"It's a looking glass. Didn't you ever read Through the Looking Glass, and What Alice Found There?"

"No. Mrs. Martin, my teacher, says we read that next year. What's a looking glass?"

"You can go through it, and into a magic world. When we go through it, the stuff in my room comes to life."

"Billy, you're not just blue. You're just plain weird!"

"C'mon," he said. He grabbed her by the arm, and yanked her off the bed. "I'll prove it to you."

He took her to the mirror, and said, "Jump!"

And they jumped.

And suddenly they were in Scotland in the 17th century. Before them was a huge castle. Beatrice couldn't believe her eyes.

"It's true!" she cried. "We went through looking glass."

"C'mon, we have to go over the moat to enter."

A drawbridge lowered, and they went over the moat.

Beatrice looked down at the water. "Are there crocs or gators in that water?" she asked. She looked scared.

"Sure there are," Billy said. "And if you embarrass me, I'll throw you down to them."

Beatrice burst into tears.

"I'm just teasing, Bee." And he hugged her.

"Beatrice, not Bee!"

"Whatever," Billy said. He rolled his eyes and let her go.

A big oak door swung open. They saw a big room with a balloon floating up near the ceiling. This was Mr. Whom, one of Billy's inventions.

"Who," Beatrice asked, are you?" Billy rolled his eyes, embarrassed already. But his little sis couldn't really be blamed. She didn't know anything about the people he had invented.

Mr. Whom's full, kind, smiling face was on the balloon.

"I," the balloon announced, "am Whom."

"Whom?" Beatrice asked.

"'Who,' not 'whom,'" Billy corrected her.

"Ah, very good!" Mr. Whom said. "If you ask 'whom' I am, that is bad grammar, even though I am Whom. Better ask 'who' I am, and then I shall reply, 'Whom.' Specifically David Whom."

[Readers, can you guess who (not whom!) Mr. Whom really is? He is a real character from history. You can research it on the Internet, or ask your parents for help. Or, if you like, you can find their real names in the appendix at the end of the book.]

"I am a famous thinker," Mr. Whom said. "And who are you two? One of you is green, and the other blue! How odd, that this should be true!"

"We are the Browns. I'm Billy. This is my sis, Bee."

"Beatrice!"

"The blue and green Browns. Billy and Bee! What a strange world it be!"

"We're neighbors of yours," Billy said. "But we live in a different century."

"Most curious. Well, if different places can be side by side, why not different times, too? Tell me, what brings you to my comfy castle?"

"First, why are you a balloon?" Beatrice blurted out.

"Well," David Whom said with a sigh, "some people think I can be a little windy."

"What does that mean?" Billy asked.

"Well, when I write, I tend to ramble on." And then he rambled on for a bit, and started running out of air. The balloon shrank toward the floor.

"I wonder if you can tell me where everything came from," Billy said. "Before you shrink into nothing."

Mr. Whom made a face. He looked confused. But the question pumped him up. He inflated again, and drifted upward.

"Tell me, too," Beatrice said.

"It's my question," Billy shot back.

"You don't own questions, Billy," she said. "Everyone owns questions. Anyone can ask any question he or she wants. Isn't that right, Mr. Whom?"

"Dad says a stork brought me and sis," Billy said. "And that God made the whole wide world."

"Ah, I see!" kindly Mr. Whom said. "You want to know why there is something rather than nothing."

"Eggs-actly," Billy said. Billy liked to pronounce "exactly" as "eggs-actly." He liked eggs in addition to liking chocolate cake. He just didn't like peas (or carrots, for that matter).

"My dad," Billy went on, "says people build houses, and the whole universe is bigger and greater than a house. So if someone built a house, someone even greater built everything. He says that someone is God."

"Hmm," said Mr. Whom. "Well, in that case, who built God, Billy?"

"Dad says no one built God. God has always been around. I guess he got bored and lonely. So he made a universe to keep him company."

"But isn't God much greater than a house?"

Billy thought about it. "I guess so," he said, after a while.

"So then someone must have built God, right?"

Billy looked deflated, while Whom the balloon inflated some more. "I guess so," Billy said, "only … only then, the builder of God would have to have a builder, too. Then his builder would have to have a builder, and then … "

"Billy, have you ever heard of 'infinity'?"

"I'm not sure."

"It means no beginning, and no end."

Now Billy looked confused.

"Listen, Billy," David Whom the balloon said, now swollen with inflated thought. He drifted up toward the ceiling. "You've seen people build houses, right? Or at least read or heard about them doing that. Have you ever seen anyone build a universe?"

"I ... I guess not," Billy said.

"Well, then, maybe no one built it at all."

"I'm bored," Beatrice complained.

"Buzz off, Bee," Billy said.

"No, you buzz off, Billy Brain!" And she stuck her tongue out at him.

"Children!" Whom the balloon cried. "You're giving this balloon high air pressure!"

"Maybe we'll go visit more neighbors and see what they have to say," Billy Brain told Whom the Balloon.

"Oh, take me with you!" David Whom said. "I'd like to meet the neighbors, too."

So Billy took Whom the Balloon by his string, and off they went.

Mr. Sour Hour the vulture

Chapter Three

They went to visit cranky old Mr. Sour Hour in his 19th-century haunted house. It was full of black bats. And not just black bats — there were black cats, too. There were bats and cats and both were black. Sometimes the cats ate the bats. Sometimes the bats ate the cats. But both the cats and the bats were black.

Mr. Sour Hour looked just like a vulture. In fact, he *was* a vulture. And who would look more like a vulture, than a vulture? Billy Brain was always surprised to learn new things about the people he had made up.

"It sure is scary in here," Beatrice whispered. Mr. Sour Hour had answered the door knocker and let them in. He said, "Who in the world would want to visit an old crank like me? And who is this balloon?" There were cobwebs everywhere.

"This balloon," said Billy, "is Whom."

"Who?"

"Whom!"

"Oh — David Whom! Yes, I recognize you, now. Some of your work influenced me. You see, I may be a vulture. But I am also a philosopher."

"What's a philosopher?" Billy asked.

"Someone who thinks really hard about the world," both the balloon and vulture said.

"I'm afraid I haven't had the pleasure of making your acquaintance," Mr. Whom told the vulture. "Billy here tells me your name is Sour Hour?"

"Well, something like that. [See the appendix for the real person behind the character. Or, research it on your own.] My first name is Arthur. Arthur Sour Hour. Now what do you people want?" Mr. Sour Hour sounded sour at this early hour.

"We're your neighbors."

"I don't like neighbors. I don't like visitors. I prefer to stay shut up in my house with my bats and my cats."

"I want to know who I am, and why I'm here," Billy said.

"A cop once asked me that while I was strolling in the park," the vulture said. He clacked his beak. "'Who are you?'" he asked. "'Why are you here?'" And I said: "Ah! Those are the questions, aren't they?"

"Well?" Beatrice said boldly. "What are the answers?"

"I have my own question first," the old crank said. "Why are you kids blue and green?"

"Who knows!" the kids said. Billy added: "I'm beginning to think I don't know anything."

"That's not true, Billy," David Whom said. "You know why building a house is a false analogy for building a universe."

"Analogy?" Billy asked.

"A kind of comparison," Mr. Whom said.

"Oh," Billy said, with a smile. "Right."

"Who are we?" the vulture parroted. "Why are we here?"

"And why is this place so gloomy?" Beatrice asked.

"Bee, shut up," Billy said.

"No, you shut up!"

"You!"

"Gloomy? Gloomy?" Mr. Sour Hour produced a half-filled cup of water. "Is it half full? Or half empty?"

Before anyone could reply, Mr. Sour Hour said: "It's half empty. Why? Because I'm a pessimist."

"Pess …" Billy began, "pess …"

"PESS-I-MIST" Arthur Sour Hour said. "It means I look on the dark side of things!" And the old bird cackled.

"You really are a Gloomy Gus," Beatrice boldly replied. "I bet you don't get invited to many parties." Billy giggled in spite of himself. Whom the balloon smiled. He may have been windy, but he got invited to parties!

"Parties," the old bird scoffed, "are for happy people. Everyone is sad. And if you're not sad, then you should be!"

"I don't feel sad," Beatrice said.

"You should feel sad."

"But I don't!"

"So, what about it?" Billy asked. "Who are we? Why are we here?"

"Who knows!" the old bird exclaimed. "Just like who knows why you kids are blue and green!"

"But did the whole world have a beginning? And if so, was there a creator? And if not, how could a whole world exist without being made? Or having begun?"

"A beginning! A middle! An end! In other words, time! Just what do you think time is, young man?"

"Well, there's bed time, dinner time …"

"Time! Time and space are part of the world of appearances. They are not real."

"What is real, then?"

"The will. The thing in itself. Everything else is just — mere representation!"

"What do you mean by will?" the kids asked.

"A will is a striving — you know, the will to do chores, so you can get an allowance."

"I hate chores," Billy sulked.

A "representation," he explained, is like a drawing. The drawing of a dog represents a dog, but is not the dog.

"Time — and everything else — are like waves on the ocean," Mr. Sour Hour said. "The ocean — by this analogy — is the thing in itself. The ocean's water is the will. And the waves are its representation."

"You remember what 'analogy' means, right, Billy?" Mr. Whom asked.

"Sure," Billy beamed.

"Me, too," Beatrice said.

"Another way to look at 'will' or 'willing' is this: Acting according to a concept. So if you kids go to math class, pay attention, and do your work, you are 'willing' a concept: an education."

Billy made a face. "I don't like math," he said.

Beatrice said, "Those are strange ideas. Does anyone else believe them?"

"Truth passes through three stages. First, it is ridiculed. Then it is opposed. Then it is accepted as self-evident." He thought for a moment and added, "Well, except on Twitter. I mean, X. Any bullpucky goes there."

"I'm hungry!" Billy shouted.

"Maybe we should all have a bite to eat," Mr. Whom said. "Even a balloon can use extra air."

"Are you eating out?" Mr. Sour Hour asked. "Do you mind if I go with you? Sometimes even a vulture needs company. Besides, I find you people interesting. And I get sick of eating carrion."

"Carry-on?" Beatrice asked. "Like carry-on luggage at the airport? You eat luggage, Mr. Sour Hour?"

Mr. Whom said quickly, "Don't worry about that right now, Beatrice." He didn't want her to know that "carrion" means "rotting flesh." So he asked her: "What would you like to eat?"

"Let's go to McDonald's!" the girl said. "I want to get a Happy Meal!" Talk about rotting flesh! Well, OK, at least it's cooked.

So they all went off to McDonald's.

Mr. Knee Cheese on his nag

Chapter Four

It was a nice McDonald's. It was special. It had golden arches. But all McDonald's have golden arches, don't they? So maybe it wasn't so special after all.

But wait! There was one thing special about it. The prices.

When they all entered, Billy Brain was surprised to see Mr. Knee Cheese at the counter. He was ordering lunch. The young man behind the counter had pimples. He said to Mr. Knee Cheese, "You want fries with that?"

"Jawohl!" Mr. Knee Cheese snapped. That's a fancy German way of saying "Yes." There are a number of Germans in this story.

The young man rang up the purchase and said, "Eighteen dollars, please."

"Eighteen dollars! For a Big Mac, fries, and a soft drink! Are you mad?"

The young man shrugged and said, "Inflation." Then he picked at a pimple. Inflation means rising prices. "Anyhow, folks say you're mad," the kid said.

Mr. Knee Cheese grumbled and threw down some bills. The others made their orders. Billy had to buy for everyone with him. He had brought some birthday dough his aunt had sent him. The others were broke. You know how philosophers are. They think hard about stuff, except how to pay the bills.

They asked if the could join Mr. Knee Cheese at his table.

The pet walrus above his lips stirred. Mr. Knee Cheese's horse was tied up outside. It was like something out of the old West.

"If you insist," Mr. Knee Cheese said.

"Who is this guy, anyway?" Beatrice whispered to Billy.

"I'm pretty sure he's another German philosopher," Billy said.

"Boy, you German philosophers sure are grumpy," Beatrice told Mr. Knee Cheese.

But they all sat down and got to talking.

"Is your name really Knee Cheese?" Billy asked.

"Frederich Knee Cheese." [You can find the real man behind the name in the appendix, kids.]

Mr. Sour Hour took a bite of his cheeseburger and made a funny face — a sour face. The vulture said, "I think I prefer carrion."

Beatrice said in a side whisper to the guy with the walrus above his lips, "He likes to eat people's baggage."

"Baggage!" Mr. Knee Cheese said. "We all carry baggage from the past! Like the baggage of God!"

Billy said, "Mr. Knee Cheese, did God make the world?"

"Got ist tot!"

"What's that mean?"

"It's German for, 'God is dead,' Billy," Mr. Whom the balloon said. He was drifting on his string above their table. Some people thought he was a McDonald's decoration. A big figurine of Ronald McDonald was lounging on a bench. He was grinning at the balloon.

"Really?"

"And we killed him," Mr. Knee Cheese said.

"That's awful!" Beatrice cried. She was sad.

"How'd we do that?" Billy asked.

"We began to refuse to believe in him."

"Mom and Dad both believe in him," Billy and Beatrice Brain said together.

"Some people don't want to hear the truth because they don't want their illusions destroyed."

"But don't we go to heaven when we die?"

"In heaven, all the interesting people are missing."

"Mom and Dad like to praise God."

"I cannot believe in a God who wants to be praised all the time." He munched on his fries and said, "These fries stink! Too much salt."

"But if we don't go to heaven when we die, where do we go?" Beatrice was worried about this.

"Maybe you live your life over and over again, little girl," Mr. Knee Cheese said. "Have you ever thought of that?"

"No! What a strange idea!"

"Like a video game," Billy said. "A character on screen disappears off the right side, and comes back on the left."

"Remarkable idea," Mr. Whom the balloon said, as he bobbed up by the ceiling.

"I call it the eternal recurrence," said the guy who couldn't stand his fries.

Billy looked puzzled. Mr. Whom told him: "Eternal means forever. To recur means to happen again. To happen again and again forever."

"My idea," the old Sour Hour vulture said, "is that the individual dies, but the will goes on. When one water ripple fades out, the ocean — the will — makes another."

"But I sure would hate to have to eat these fries forever and ever," Mr. Knee Cheese said glumly. "There is that."

Billy said, "You're saying time goes in circles?"

"Is the earth flat or a ball?"

"A ball."

"Then why, when I look down the street, does it look flat?"

"Because any circle looks straight if it's big enough."

"Right! Now, time seems flat. But maybe that is just like looking a little way down the street. Maybe if you look far enough, it curves around again. Like the earth."

Billy thought hard about that. He said, "Maybe." Then he looked out the window and said, "What's with the horse?"

Mr. Knee Cheese sighed. "Long story short: some terrible man was whipping that horse. I threw my arms around it to protect it. It's one reason people say my knees are made of cheese. My knees buckled while I saved the horse. It's also why people say I'm crazy. Because I saved a horse."

"That doesn't sound crazy," Beatrice said. "That sounds sweet." And she gave him a peck on the cheek.

"Thank you, little girl." He smiled broadly. It made the walrus bark. "Incidentally, why are you green, and the boy —"

"My brother."

"Why is your brother blue?"

Billy sighed and said, "We don't know."

"But it makes you two special, I bet."

"I guess." But Billy didn't sound happy about it.

"Special is a good thing," Mr. Knee Cheese said. "Imagine how boring life would be if everyone were the same. You know, like herd of cattle."

"But isn't there safety in a herd?" Billy asked.

"Safety, but sameness and dullness. I advocate the will to power."

"What's that?" Beatrice asked.

"Overcoming yourself. To overcome a thing blocking you. To do that, you must overcome your own limits."

"Like overcoming peas," Billy suggested.

"Of these awful fries, I suppose," Mr. Knee Cheese said. "But when you overcome, you live exactly the life you want. And then, you will be happy to have the exact same life over and over."

"The Eternal Recurrence," Beatrice said.

"Exactly!"

Soon they finished lunch. Crumbs lay on the table, and the walrus above Mr. Knee Cheese's lips lunged down and ate them up. Then it barked.

Billy wanted to continue touring the neighborhood. He invited Mr. Knee Cheese to tag along. He agreed, and off they went. Mr. Knee Cheese saddled up his horse. Mr. Sour Hour spread his wings. Mr. Whom drifted along with the air currents. The walrus, fat and happy from the crumbs, barked, whistled and chirped. It rode on Mr. Knee Cheese's face. Billy and Beatrice went the old-fashioned way. They walked.

Mr. Darwinkle the moose

Chapter Five

But then they came to some water, and Billy and Beatrice couldn't walk anymore. So they rode on the wings of Mr. Sour Hour the vulture. Mr. Whom the balloon drifted above the water. Mr. Knee Cheese forded the water with his horse.

Suddenly they were on an island. They were introduced to Mr. Darwinkle, a wrinkled old moose with a beard. [Who is he really? You can find out!]

He was surrounded by the Doppelgängers. They were all exactly alike, except they weren't.

"I don't understand," Billy said. "They all look exactly alike, except they're different."

"That's right!" Mr. Darwinkle said. "Just like you and your girlfriend —"

"Sister."

"Sister! Even better! You are directly related. You both have two eyes, two arms, two legs, a mouth, a nose, and hair. But you are a boy and she is a girl. And — what's better — is that you are blue, and she is green."

"But why?"

"Natural selection. At least in part. There may be other reasons. I don't know all of it. I live in the 19th century, you see. But others will find out more after I am gone."

"What's natural selection?"

"Like the Doppelgängers, everything reproduces, Billy. But there are little tiny differences when they do. Sometimes those differences help the living thing survive. If they do, that trait spreads into future generations. That's how new animals arise from old animals."

"I thought God made all living things," Beatrice said.

"Well, maybe he did. But he used natural change over time to make new animals and plants out of older ones. It's called evolution."

"But Doppelgängers are made up!" Beatrice said. "Look, they all have four coat-button eyes, potato noses, big old claws, and furry wings! They are all alike, but different. The wings are different sizes. Those noses are big or small. Some claws are more curved than others. But that's because they are all in the mind. Billy, you made them up!"

Suddenly the Doppelgängers tap-danced on cloven hooves. They waved around canes, and black top hats over their heads. They burst into song:

Doppelgängers, 'tis what we awes,
Differsame and yet sameferrent,
'tater noses, furry wings, big ol' claws,
four button eyes, 'tis our element.

Whickerwalkers, jabbertalkers,
Busybodies, freakydees,
Island dwellers, geeky stalkers,
We ford the waters, and climb up trees.

With grand ol' Darwinkle, beardy moose,
We sciencefied a revolution:
Plantimals, moocow and mongoose,
Monkeys, too, all from evolution.

We are the Doppelgängers, gängers, gängers
We are the Doppelgängers, gängers, gängers
We don't wibble or waffle, we're not awful.
We Doppel! Gängers! Gängers! Gängers!

Four button eyes, 'tis our element.
'tater noses, furry wings, big ol' claws,
Differsame and yet sameferrent,
Doppelgängers, 'tis what we awes.

"That's not bad, for made-up beings," Beatrice said.

"I thought it sucked," Billy said.

"Billy! What would mom say at such language?"

Billy shrugged. "Mom's not here."

Deflated, the Doppelgängers dropped their top hats and canes. Then they settled down into a glum pile and moped.

"Don't quit you day job," Billy told the Doppelgängers.

Then he turned to Mr. Darwinkle.

"But you're really a moose," Billy said. "Not made up. A moose with a big old white beard. Why aren't you a human?"

"That's so interesting, Billy. Because people are actually related to moose. You are, too. They are like our distant relatives. We share a common ancestor with them. But it goes way, way back in time."

"But you moose all DO look the same," Beatrice said. "Not like those weird Doppelgängers."

"Do we now?" Mr. Darwinkle smiled. "Tell me what do you see about me?"

"Well, you have a beard, and big antlers and your eyes are blue, I think."

"Very good, Beatrice, now, look at my moose friend over there. What do you see?"

Beatrice squinted her eyes. "He has smaller antlers, brown eyes, and no beard."

"Exactly!" Mr. Darwinkle exclaimed, "Now look at that island next to us. Look at the moose there. What do you see?"

Beatrice leaned forward.

"Um, they look the same … well, no. Their feet look different. Bigger and flatter."

"Ah, Beatrice. See what you notice, when you look closely?"

Billy had been squinting and looking along with Beatrice.

"And on that other island," he said, "the moose all have really big ears!"

"When you look real hard, the wonders of the natural world will come out."

"So it's not just the made-up Doppelgängers," Beatrice said. "It's the moose, too."

"And you, too, so true, so true! One of you is green, and the other blue!"

Billy said, "We're trying to figure out where everything came from."

"Well," Mr. Darwinkle said, "That's where new kinds of animals — they're called 'species' — come from. How life began, no one knows."

"God did it!" Beatrice spoke up.

The walrus above Mr. Knee Cheese's lips wiggled, chirped, and barked. It often did this when Mr. Knee Cheese was about to say something important. It was like how some people clear their throats before speaking.

"You know what they say about priests," the horse lover said. "Into every gap they put their delusions, their stopgap, which they call God."

"What's a delusion?" the kids wanted to know.

"A strong belief in something false," Mr. Whom and Mr. Sour Hour said.

Beatrice looked sad. "Doesn't anybody believe in God but me and Mom and Dad?"

"Certainly you may believe in God," Mr. Whom the balloon exhaled. "But what you are learning, child, is that reality is more complicated than simple answers can explain."

"If there is a God, he shouldn't have made life at all." That was Mr. Sour Hour. He was sour again. "It would have been better if he had left the earth dead. Like the moon."

"You know, sometimes you're a real downer," Mr. Whom told Mr. Sour Hour.

Mr. Sour Hour gave Mr. Whom the raspberry.

"Let's explore some more," Billy said. "It's such an interesting neighborhood I live in! This is way more interesting than school. In school, the teachers make us remember stuff. Like facts, figures, and dates. And the multiplication tables. It's so boring. As soon as I remember the facts, I forget them. When the test is over. I remember so much I forget it all! But I won't forget this stuff."

They invited Mr. Darwinkle and the Doppelgängers to come along, and they agreed. And off they went.

The Invisible Pink Unicorn

Chapter Six

Now they went to see Mr. Kalamazoo. As mentioned, he was not really a person, but a way of thinking He was also a city in Michigan. But more, he was a medieval scholar. Scholar kind of means "wise guy." He kept an invisible pink unicorn as a pet. "Medieval" means the Middle Ages. That was hundreds of years ago. He was also a Muslim. Muslims are different from Christians, but both believe in God. Christians and Muslims are sort of like the Doppelgängers. They're alike, but different.

He lived in a mosque. A mosque is a Muslim temple. It's like a church, only different. It was a beautiful mosque. It had nice minarets, which are towers, and a lot of arches. Inside the ceilings were covered with wonderful designs. They were made of colored tiles. Many were symmetrical. That means exactly similar parts facing each other, or around a central point. Like snowflakes. Or like Doppelgängers, in a way.

When they introduced one another, Billy learned that "Kalamazoo" means "speech," "word," or "utterance." The word of Allah, or God. [Of course, that's not the real name of this way of thinking. See if you can figure it out.]

"What's with the invisible pink unicorn?" Beatrice wanted to know.

"Well," Mr. Kalamazoo replied, "she's pink, but invisible. So it's hard to say she's really pink. Plus, she's a unicorn — an animal like a small horse, with a single horn. But unicorns don't exist. She can't be both pink and invisible, and unicorns don't exist. Maybe it's best not to speak of her at all."

"I don't get it," Billy said.

"Well, some people say God is like that. That he exists, but can't be seen. Or heard. Or smelled. Or touched. Or tasted."

"Does that mean God doesn't exist?" Beatrice looked glum.

"Not at all," Mr. Kalamazoo replied. "Consider:

1. Everything that begins to exist, has a cause of its existence.
2. The universe began to exist.
3. Therefore, the universe had a cause of its existence."

Mr. Whom the balloon looked unconvinced. He said: "And that cause is — your invisible pink unicorn?"

"Well, maybe. But a better idea is this: the cause is God."

"And what caused God to exist?" Mr. Sour Hour wanted to know.

"Nothing! That's the beauty of it. Only things that BEGIN to exist have a cause. God never began to exist. That is because he is outside time. And outside space. He just is!"

"Well," Mr. Whom said, "Your invisible pink unicorn never began to exist, either. Why? Because she doesn't exist at all!"

"But God does!"

"How do you know the universe began to exist?" Mr. Darwinkle asked. "Maybe the universe has always existed. Maybe IT just is, not God."

"Well, life began to exist, right?"

"Yes."

"Well, if life began to exist, then the universe, which contains life, must also have begun to exist. Plus, it is impossible to have an infinite past time."

"But God — or maybe your invisible pink unicorn — must also have had an infinite past time, then. Because you say she did not begin to exist."

"No," Mr. Kalamazoo said. "God exists OUTSIDE time. So he did not NEED to begin to exist."

The two philosophers and the scientist did not seem convinced. Billy Brain was fascinated. Beatrice frowned.

"I have to think about this," she said. "My head hurts a little. I'd like some candy — and a root beer float!"

"I know!" Billy cried. "Let's go visit Mr. Eins Stein, in the sky! 'Eins Stein' means 'one glass.' We can get one glass of root beer from him."

"Just one?" Beatrice asked.

"It's a BIG glass," Billy assured her. "We can each use a straw."

They invited Mr. Kalamazoo and his invisible pink unicorn to go with them. They all closed their eyes, thought real hard, and then blasted off into outer space. That is where Mr. One Glass lived. He orbited the earth in a great big flying saucer.

Mr. Ein Stein in his flying saucer

Chapter Seven

There was a young lady named Bright
Whose speed was far faster than light;
She set out one day
In a relative way
And returned on the previous night.

"We don't get that at all," everyone told Mr. Eins Stein. He was floating in his flying saucer orbiting the earth. All the others were floating, too. They were in the saucer with him, in free fall. When in outer space, you don't feel gravity, though it is still there. That's why the ship orbits the earth: gravity.

"Yes," the guy who wore no socks said. His first name, they learned, was Albert. [In addition to wearing no socks, he was a famous scientist in real life. Try to guess who he is!] "Except I came after all of you. That's why I know stuff you don't. Well, after all of you, except for you and your sister, Billy." They had already introduced one another.

Mr. Eins Stein asked the boy, "Have you learned about my relativity idea yet?"

"Not yet."

"Of course not. You are too young."

"What is your idea?"

"Time is relative. Example: put your hand on a hot stove for a minute, and it seems like an hour. Sit with a pretty girl for an hour, and it seems like a minute. That's relativity!" The old scientist cackled.

No one laughed.

Beatrice was sad. She said, "Does talking with me seem like an hour?"

"Oh, no!" the absent-minded professor who wore no socks said. "With you, it seems like less than a second, young lady!"

Beatrice was happy again.

Mr. Whom the balloon huffed, "Are you off your rocker, old man?"

So the old scientist tried to explain. He did this especially after he listened to Mr. Kalamazoo talk about his ideas of time. One of his ideas was that there could not be an infinite past. So the universe had to have a beginning.

"Well," Mr. Eins Stein said, "What IS time?"

"It seems to flow," Mr. Sour Hour said. "Like a river. From past to future. Of course, that is the representation of time."

"That's right! The representation! But the map is not the land. It's just the map."

"Yes," the old vulture cackled.

"Couldn't we also say that you stand still in time, and the future flows back toward you? In that way, it becomes the present?"

"Maybe," they all agreed.

"Or maybe time just IS. It doesn't flow at all."

"How do you mean?" they all asked.

"Maybe time is like space. It's all there, just like space is all there. Only, some things are earlier than other things. And some things are later. The things that are not earlier, and not later, we call 'the present.'"

They listened.

"Just like one city can be east of another city. And a different city can be west of the same city. But all three cities exist. Whatever city we are in, we call it 'here.' Whatever time we are in, we call it 'now.'"

They waited.

"Whether you are east or west, or in the middle, is relative. It depends on where you stand. The same with earlier, later, and the present. It depends on when you stand."

They told him to go on.

"But we — well, I, because I am a genius — discovered that time (and space) are 'relative' in another way. Say someone travels really fast. Then he turns around and comes back. When he does, and rejoins you, less time has passed on his clock, than on yours."

"No way!" they all said.

"Way!" Mr. Eins Stein said. "And someone sitting on the surface of the earth ages more slowly than someone on a mountain. That is because time passes slower where gravity is more strongly felt, as on the surface. However, because I am whipping around the earth at a high rate of speed, I still age even more slowly than people on the ground."

They could not find words to say.

"But listen — it's complicated! I'm just trying to give you a taste of it. One must take baby steps to learn hard stuff. Take it a little bit at a time. Like a seed. This is a seed. Later, when you are older, you will have the flower."

"What does all that have to do with the lady named Bright?" they asked.

"Well, the speed of light is very, VERY fast. But it turns out light is a SPEED LIMIT. Nothing can travel as fast, or faster, than it. As you speed up, and get close to the speed of light, less time passes for you, than for someone standing still relative to you."

They waited.

"If you could travel AT the speed of light — time would STOP!"

"How do you know?"

"You see, not only is light very fast, its speed is the same for all people who measure it. Think about it. If I am riding on a beam of light, the light from a clock behind me could never catch up with the light I am riding. The clock would be frozen. No time would pass!"

"And if you could go faster than light? Would you really travel backward in time, like that Bright lady?"

"Well, not exactly. That is just a funny limerick. What would happen, though, is that from certain points of view, you would see events happen before their causes."

"You're joking."

"No, it's no joke. But Billy and Beatrice, I'm just given you a TASTE of this. Just like a taste of this root beer." He had produced a HUGE root beer float. They were all drinking from the same eins stein with different straws. "You're still kids. You'll learn more about this in high school. Just keep what I said in mind for now."

"WE'RE not kids," Mr. Whom, Mr. Sour Hour and Mr. Darwinkle protested. "And we don't get it, either."

"No, you're not, but you came BEFORE me. You'll need to catch up."

"But what does this have to do with why everything exists?" It was Mr. Kalamazoo speaking. "What does it have to do with my proof that God exists because the universe began to exist? And that God created it?"

"Suppose past, present, and future all exist. All moments in time exist, like all places in space. Then, what we call 'the first moment' is just another moment in time. To ask, 'What came before the first moment in time?' makes no sense. It would be like asking, 'What is north of the north pole?' There can BE no 'north of the north pole.' From there, everything is SOUTH. So too from the First Moment. There can be no BEFORE the first moment. No 'earlier than.' Everything is LATER THAN the first moment."

"And the First Moment doesn't need a cause?" Mr. Kalamazoo asked.

"Of course not. No more than the north pole needs a cause. It just IS. Just like all times just ARE, when they ARE."

Beatrice asked: "Doesn't that mean you ALWAYS exist — between the time you were born, and the time you die?"

"Why, yes," the absent-minded professor said. "I guess so. Which means I'll have all the time I need to find my socks. I guess I forgot to put them in the sock drawer."

"Zounds!" Mr. Knee Cheese exclaimed. The walrus on his upper lip barked and did a black flip. "That IS my ETERNAL RECURRENCE!"

"You mean about my socks? My socks never seen to recur."

"No! About always existing between your birth and death!"

"Maybe," Mr. Eins Stein said. "For us practicing physicists, the distinction between past, present and future is a stubbornly persistent illusion."

They all waited.

"Now," the absent-minded professor said, "Let's have more root beer!"

And they had a root beer float party. That made sense, since they were in free fall, and all were floating!

Mr. Free Throw

Chapter Eight

Mr. Eins Stein agreed to give them all a ride on his flying saucer. They whizzed around the earth. They saw what a great, big, beautiful ball our home in space is. Soon they were home again, touring the neighborhood again.

They dropped in on Mr. Free Throw. Billy liked basketball. He hoped Mr. Throw would show him a thing or two about scoring.

"Well," the ancient Greek philosopher told him, "that's not exactly my name — but close enough." [Remember, readers, you can find out who he really is!] He added, "To be honest, I don't really play basketball. I don't even know what it is!"

"Oh," Billy sad, looking sad. "Guess I goofed."

"Goofball!" his sister teased.

"Pea brain!" Billy returned.

They began to wrestle. The others broke them up.

"Heavens, children!" Mr. Whom the balloon huffed and puffed. "That's not good behavior. Not at all!"

"What is the good?" Mr. Free Throw asked. Nobody asks this before actually tossing a free throw, please note.

"That's easy," Beatrice said. "God wants what is good."

"Hmm," Mr. Free Throw replied. "So God wants the good because it is good?"

"I guess," Beatrice said. But she sounded unsure.

"I smell a trick," Billy said under his breath.

"Or is it good, because God wants it?"

"I knew it," Billy said.

Beatrice began to understand.

"That kind of makes no sense," she said after a while. "If God wants the good because it IS good ... but if it's only good because God wants it ..."

"That's called 'circular reasoning,' Beatrice," Mr. Whom said. He sounded kindly. "It means you end up where you start. As a result, you get nowhere."

"I get it!" Beatrice cried. "It's like when Grandpa Simpson keeps putting on and taking off his hat, and walking in and out the door. Over and over again!"

"Um ... if you say so, child," Mr. Whom, confused, said. The poor balloon and never seen a Simpsons TV episode before.

"Well," Billy said. "At least that means there is a God. That means there was a creator."

"Not so fast, Billy," Mr. Sour Hour chimed in. "Even if God created the good — which means the good is his whim — it doesn't mean he created everything."

"Not only that," Mr. Darwinkle said, "but we have another explanation for the good. Remember how I talked about evolution? Good behavior evolved."

"How do you mean?" Billy and Beatrice Brain asked together.

"Remember how I said certain traits can help animals survive better? Certain behaviors can, too. Cooperation, friendliness, loyalty — those things help animals that work together, like humans, do better. And when the do better, they call those things 'good.'"

Now Beatrice smelled a rat.

"You know," she said, "that sounds a bit like Grandpa Simpson, too."

"Maybe so," Mr. Darwinkle said. "But it's still an explanation of where what we call 'good' came from. Even if it is still a bit circular. You know, maybe sometimes, circular definitions are the best we can do."

"I know! Mr. Eins Stein cried. He was feeling a bit jolly from too much root beer. "Let's forget all this thinking for a while, and take a break. In other words, let's blow this popcorn stand! Thinking is hard! I should know! Instead, let's blast off, and take a tour of the universe!" And so they did. They intended to party hearty into the starry void!

Some female philosphers

Chapter Nine

Mr. Eins Stein was about to yank the super-duper overdrive tiller to blast them into Warp Drive 50. But Beatrice put her foot down.

"Just a darned minute!" she said. "All the people in this neighborhood are MEN. Well, and my brother, who is a boy."

"Watch who you're calling a boy, Buzz Breath!"

"Where are the women thinkers?"

"You mean girls?" Billy asked. He was shocked. "I didn't put any girls in my neighborhood. Girls have cooties!"

"Nonsense, Billy," the others corrected. Then they told Billy and Beatrice that there have been plenty of great women thinkers. Only, history often overlooks them. Why? Because it always overlooks the contributions of women and girls.

"Let me show you," Mr. Eins Stein said. He switched on the onboard computer. Then he did a Google search. "Here are ten good ones right here," he said. They watched the names scroll by.

Hannah Arendt
Simone de Beauvoir
Mary Wollstonecraft
Hypatia
Rosa Luxemburg
Helena Blavatsky
Susan Sontag
Simone Weil
Juana Inez del a Cruz
Iris Murdoch

"And that's just to name ten, from different times," Mr. Eins Stein said. "There are hundreds — thousands — of others."

"So we women get the short end of the stick," Beatrice pouted.

"You're a girl, not a woman," Billy said.

"Watch who you're calling a girl, Blue Boy!"

"Phht!"

"Life is unfair," Mr. Sour Hour said.

"Boys get it too," Billy said. He looked really unhappy, suddenly.

"What's the matter, Billy?" the others asked.

"People tease me because I have a big brain. And because my skin is blue. I try not to show it, but sometimes it bothers me."

"You're not alone!" Beatrice cried. "I'm smart, too, and sometimes the kid call me 'Brain.' Then plus my skin is green. No one else has green skin. And I'm a girl! They make fun of me for that, too! Even you make fun of me for being a girl. And I'm your own sister." She burst into tears. Billy began crying, too.

The others consoled the children.

"Like I told you earlier," Mr. Knee Cheese said. "It's GOOD to be different — to be unique — to be yourself! Who wants to be part of a dull herd! Everyone like everyone like everyone else! Bah! What a poor world that would be. You two children are the difference makers!"

Hearing this, the kids cheered up.

"I'm sorry if I tease you sometimes, Bee," Billy told Beatrice.

"I'm sorry if I tease you sometimes, too, Billy," Beatrice said. "Once you said you thought I was jealous of you. Actually, you're my hero!"

"Really?"

"Really!"

"And you can call me Bee, if you like. I don't mind."

"Really?"

"Really!"

"As to the women thinkers, you'll meet then when you get older," Mr. Whom said. "As long as you stay in school, and keep up your studies. And above all, be yourselves!"

Now Billy and Beatrice Brain were positively happy again.

The Doppelgängers tap-danced and sang again, while waving about their canes and top hats. Mr. Darwinkle kept time, stomping a hoof.

Mr. Knee Cheese's walrus did a backflip on his upper lip. His horse whinnied.

Mr. Whom bobbed about near the ceiling of the ship. He was puffed up with joy.

Even Mr. Sour Hour, the sour old vulture, beat his wings in glee.

Mr. Free Throw did free throws — Billy had taught him how.

Mr. Eins Stein finally found his socks. Well, one of them. The other had been eaten by the drier.

Mr. Kalamazoo was surprised when his pet invisible pink unicorn appeared. It wasn't pink. It wasn't a unicorn. It wasn't even a she. It was nothing at all. So maybe we shouldn't say it appeared. How can nothing appear?

"You still suck," Billy told the Doppelgängers.

And with that, they really did blast off to party hearty in the starry void! All except the Doppelgängers.

They moped.

"Incidentally," Mr. Eins Stein asked the kids. "Why is one of you blue, and the other green?"

"We still don't know," Billy and Beatrice said together. "But now we don't care. We like being different!"

Homage to Planets and Orbits

Chapter Ten

Hey, kids, what follows is a poem. And the art on the previous page is called abstract art.

Poetry can be strange. It's not really about giving information. It's about making you feel something. Some kind of emotion. Poems contain word pictures. They contain sometimes odd twists of language. They can be a challenge.

Same thing with abstract art. It is not intended as an image of something real, in the real world. It's meant to give you a feeling about something. I call the art at left Homage to Planets and Orbits.

"Homage" means "respect and honor." The art is intended to make you think, or feel about stuff like planets, and their orbits. The planets are constantly sweeping around a central point, the sun.

The following poem was inspired by a poem by Arthur Rimbaud. He was French, and lived in the 19th century. His name is pronounced "ART-tur RAM-Bow."

He wrote his poem when he was just 15 years old. It started his poetry career. It was about a boy playing with a toy boat. He imagines sailing the seven seas in the boat, and all the wonderful adventures that await him.

Here I write about our heroes blasting off into outer space and touring the wonders of the universe, before returning home. I have made it poetical to avoid dry facts. I hope to make the reader feel wonder and awe.

Maybe puzzlement, too. Some word are pretty big. You may have to use a dictionary. Some parts may not be easy to understand. But try to work through it.

Afterward, you will find the Rimbaud poem that inspired this poem. It is called "The Drunken Boat." The word "Drunken" is used as stand-in for wild happiness. It does NOT mean you should drink! You shouldn't. (Well, milk is OK).

Remember, you can be a poet, a writer, an artist, or a musician as well. You don't have to have an ordinary job. It's fine to be a fireman, a police officer, a construction worker, or a businessman. The world needs them.

But it also needs poets, writers, artists, musicians, and thinkers. Chase whatever dream makes you happy. Have you ever read a book called Frederick, by Leo Leoni? It's about a field mouse who is different from all the other mice. While they gather nuts, wheat, and straw, he gathers rainbows, colors, and words. At first, he seems like an outcast. But later, all those things come in handy.

Also remember what Mr. Knee Cheese said: You don't have to be part of a herd. Different is good! And that's true whether your skin is blue, green, white, black, brown, or any other shade of the rainbow.

Beyond the Infinite

As I was flying down Minkowski's spacetime river,
I no longer felt myself guided by navigators;
Yelping red Martians had taken them as targets
And had nailed them naked to constellations in the sky.

I was indifferent to all crews,
The bearer of asteroid ore or the moon's helium,
When with my navigators this uproar stopped.
The worldtube paths let me go where I wanted.

In the furious flashing of the stars
More heedless than AI brains of the other era,
I shot! And loosened planets
Have not undergone a more triumphant blastoff.

The solar winds blessed my spacetime vigils;
In Zero G I danced on the skies
That are called eternal rollers of time,
Ten thousand nights, without missing the stupid eye of Jupiter!

Harsher than the prick of the suspended animation needle
The radioactivity penetrated my hull of metal and flesh
And ravaged me with spots of blue cancer
And my vomit, scattering stars and planets alike.

And from then on I bathed in the Poem of the Sky,
Infused with stars and the incandescent,
Devouring the azure worlds; where, like pale elated
Celestial flotsam, a lost astronaut sometimes floats;

Where, suddenly dyeing the starry blackness, delirium
And slow rhythms under the streaking of vagabond daylights,
Stronger than rocket fuel, vaster than our Canaveral pyres,
The bitter redness of a Martian desert ferments!

I know the skies bursting with pulsars, and the solar winds
And the star surf and their currents; I know the evening,
And a distant dawn as exalted as an opera of suns,
And at times I have seen what a spaceman thought he saw!

I have seen the low sun spotted with magnetic field flux
That inhibits convection, lighting up, with long licking arcs,
Resembling actors of very ancient dramas,
The gravity waves rolling far off their quivering of stutters!

I have dreamed of the blue night with Pluto's snows,
A kiss slowly rising to the eyes of Time,
The circulation of unknown sapients,
And the yellow and blue awakening of singing aliens!

I followed during pregnant months the solar swells,
Like hysterical cosmic rays, in their assault on the stratosphere,
Without dreaming that the incandescent fleet of the fairies
Could constrain the snout of the wheezing worlds!

I struck against, you know, unbelievable Saturns
Mingling with its rings astral eyes and human
Skin! Rainbows stretched like gravity's reins
Under the horizon of Titan's ethane seas to greenish moons!

I have seen celestial Sargassos, ship traps

Where a whole Leviathan starship rots from radium!
Avalanches of nebulae in the midst of a calm,
With the relativistic distances contracting toward the abyss!

Pluto's glaciers, suns of silver, skies of embers!
Hideous strands at the ends of galactic gulfs
Where alien serpents half-devoured by AI bots
Fall down from gnarled stars eaten by black holes!

I should like to have shown children those suns
Of the galactic swirl, the worlds of gold, the singing stars.
Flicks of flares from the sun rocked my drifting
And ineffable solar winds winged me at times.

At times a martyr weary of poles and zones,
Outer space, whose silent sob rocked my gentle roll,
Brought up to me her alien puckers with yellow suckers
And I remained, like a mutant on its knees,

Resembling an asteroid tossing on my sides the quarrels
And droppings of noisy meteorites under yellow skies
And I sailed on, when through my fragile lifelines
Asphyxiated astronauts sank backward into sleep!

Now I, a starship adrift in the foliage of time,
Thrown by the solar wind into the starless void;
I whose star-drunk carcass would not have been rescued
By the Eloi or the Morlocks of H.G. Wells;

Free, smoking, wrapped in oxygen smog,
I who pierced the reddening sky like a veil,
Bearing incandescent stars for the astronomers,
Lichens of sunlight and mucus of azure,

Who flew, spotted by small electric moons,
A vagrant path, escorted by Newton's equations,
When distant novas beat down with blows of cudgels
The ultramarine skies with burning funnels;

I, who trembled, hearing at fifty light years off
The moaning of the Behemoths in heat and the thick cosmic

Maelstroms, eternal spinner of the blue immobility,
I miss the earth and its ancient imbecility!

I have seen sidereal archipelagos! And planets
Whose delirious skies are open to the astrological arpeggios;
Is it in these bottomless nights that you sleep and exile yourself,
Million golden minutes, O future vigor?

But, in truth, I have flown too much! Dawns are heartbreaking.
Every moon is atrocious and every sun bitter.
Acrid love has swollen me with intoxicating torpor
— O let my starship burst! O let me fall into the sea of space!

If I want a sky of earth, it is the blue
Summer sky where in the sweet-smelling twilight
A rising child full of sadness releases
A kite as fragile as a May butterfly.

No longer can I, bathed in your languor, O outer space,
Ride the tides of Einstein's shrunken temporality,
For I have traversed the universe in far less than a century,
But returned to an earth that has aged an $E=MC^2$ of Eternity!

Billy and Beatrice Brain — rising children full of sadness — released a kite as fragile as a May butterfly, in the sweet-smelling summer twilight. The others had brought them home just in time for dinner. The parting words of their neighbors and tour guides were these: "Never take 'because I said so' for an answer. To ANYTHING."

They had not found out why there was something rather than nothing. They still did not know the answer to the question: Where did everything come from? But now they knew something better.

They knew how to think.

"Billy and Beatrice, eat your peas," Mom and Dad said.

"Why?" the kids asked.

"Because we said so!" Mom and Dad said.

"Sorry, Mom and Dad," the kids said. "That's not good enough."

THE END

The Drunken Boat
By Arthur Rimbaud
Translated by Wallace Fowlie

As I was going down impassive Rivers,
I no longer felt myself guided by haulers:
Yelping redskins had taken them as targets
And had nailed them naked to colored stakes.

I was indifferent to all crews,
The bearer of Flemish wheat or English cottons
When with my haulers this uproar stopped
The Rivers let me go where I wanted.

Into the furious lashing of the tides
More heedless than children's brains the other winter
I ran! And loosened Peninsulas
Have not undergone a more triumphant hubbub

The storm blessed my sea vigils
Lighter than a cork I danced on the waves
That are called eternal rollers of victims,
Ten nights, without missing the stupid eye of the lighthouses!

Sweeter than the flesh of hard apples is to children
The green water penetrated my hull of fir
And washed me of spots of blue wine
And vomit, scattering rudder and grappling-hook

And from then on I bathed in the Poem
Of the Sea, infused with stars and lactescent,
Devouring the azure verses; where, like a pale elated
Piece of flotsam, a pensive drowned figure sometimes sinks;

Where, suddenly dyeing the blueness, delirium
And slow rhythms under the streaking of daylight,
Stronger than alcohol, vaster than our lyres,
The bitter redness of love ferments!

I know the skies bursting with lightning, and the waterspouts
And the surf and the currents; I know the evening,
And dawn as exalted as a flock of doves
And at times I have seen what man thought he saw!

I have seen the low sun spotted with mystic horrors,
Lighting up, with long violet clots,
Resembling actors of very ancient dramas,
The waves rolling far off their quivering of shutters!

I have dreamed of the green night with dazzled snows
A kiss slowly rising to the eyes of the sea,
The circulation of unknown saps,
And the yellow and blue awakening of singing phosphorous!

I followed during pregnant months the swell,
Like hysterical cows, in its assault on the reefs,
Without dreaming that the luminous feet of the Marys
Could constrain the snout of the wheezing Oceans!

I struck against, you know, unbelievable Floridas
Mingling with flowers panthers' eyes and human
Skin! Rainbows stretched like bridal reins
Under the horizon of the seas to greenish herds!

I have seen enormous swamps ferment, fish-traps
Where a whole Leviathan rots in the rushes!
Avalanches of water in the midst of a calm,
And the distances cataracting toward the abyss!

Glaciers, suns of silver, nacreous waves, skies of embers!
Hideous strands at the end of brown gulfs
Where giant serpents devoured by bedbugs
Fall down from gnarled trees with black scent!

I should have liked to show children those sunfish
Of the blue wave, the fish of gold, the singing fish.
— Foam of flowers rocked my drifting
And ineffable winds winged me at times.

At times a martyr weary of poles and zones,
The sea, whose sob created my gentle roll,
Brought up to me her dark flowers with yellow suckers
And I remained, like a woman on her knees...

Resembling an island tossing on my sides the quarrels
And droppings of noisy birds with yellow eyes
And I sailed on, when through my fragile ropes
Drowned men sank backward to sleep!

Now I, a boat lost in the foliage of caves,
Thrown by the storm into the birdless air
I whose water-drunk carcass would not have been rescued
By the Monitors and the Hanseatic sailboats;

Free, smoking, topped with violet fog,
I who pierced the reddening sky like a wall,
Bearing, delicious jam for good poets
Lichens of sunlight and mucus of azure,

Who ran, spotted with small electric moons,
A wild plank, escorted by black seahorses,
When Julys beat down with blows of cudgels
The ultramarine skies with burning funnels;

I, who trembled, hearing at fifty leagues off
The moaning of the Behemoths in heat and the thick Maelstroms,
Eternal spinner of the blue immobility
I miss Europe with its ancient parapets!

I have seen sidereal archipelagos! and islands
Whose delirious skies are open to the sea-wanderer:
— Is it in these bottomless nights that you sleep and exile yourself,
Million golden birds, O future Vigor?

But, in truth, I have wept too much! Dawns are heartbreaking.
Every moon is atrocious and every sun bitter.
Acrid love has swollen me with intoxicating torpor
O let my keel burst! O let me go into the sea!

If I want a water of Europe, it is the black
Cold puddle where in the sweet-smelling twilight
A squatting child full of sadness releases
A boat as fragile as a May butterfly.

No longer can I, bathed in your languor, O waves,
Follow in the wake of the cotton boats,
Nor cross through the pride of flags and flames,
Nor swim under the terrible eyes of prison ships.

Appendix

Mr. Whom the Balloon is really David Hume, the 18th-century Scottish philosopher and champion of empiricism (em-PEER-is-ism). That is the idea we need to form ideas by observation and evidence.

Mr. Sour Hour the Vulture is really Arthur Schopenhauer, the 19th century German philosopher. He thought the world of our senses was the representation of a deeper, hidden will. This will need not be that of God, though.

Mr. Knee Cheese is Friedrich Nietzsche, another 19th century German philosopher. He spoke of the death of God and the Overman, someone beyond normal standards of morality. As we have seen, he also spoke of the Eternal Recurrence.

Mr. Darwinkle the Moose is really Charles Darwin, a 19th century English naturalist and biologist. He introduced the theory of evolution, which you have learned about.

Mr. Kalamazoo represents the Kalam school that studied Islamic thought.

Mr. Eins Stein, or One Glass, is of course Albert Einstein, the 20th-century German scientist who developed the theory of relativity. You were introduced to it in this book.

Mr. Free Throw is really Euthyphro, a character made up by Plato, an ancient Greek philosopher. The character talked about the nature of morality and justice.

www.ingramcontent.com/pod-product-compliance
Lightning Source LLC
Chambersburg PA
CBHW061253040426
42444CB00010B/2370